HOW THEY LIV

TIGERS

RUPERT MATTHEWS

MALLARD PRESS

A pair of Siberian tigers, the largest of all the subspecies, drinking from a frozen stream in winter.

Contents

King of the Cats

The tiger is the most powerful and emotive symbol of the East. For centuries travellers in Asia have brought back tales of the majesty and ferocity of the tiger, the ultimate predator of the dark, luxuriant forests. It has no natural enemies and can stride its realm in safety. The echoing roars of the tiger boom out unchallenged by any animal. In the long struggle between man and nature, the tiger has taken the lead against humans. It has dominated the folklore and myths of Asia every bit as much as it dominates the wildlife.

Today's tiger is at home in the lush forests and jungles of Asia. It is most familiar to us as the predator of the steamy jungles of India and Southeast Asia. Yet this is not its original home. The oldest tiger fossils, dating back nearly a million years, have been found far to the north near the Lena River. Winding through the largely unexplored wilderness of northeastern Siberia, the Lena flows through dense coniferous forests. During the winter, temperatures plunge to well below freezing and snow blankets the land.

It was in this hostile habitat that the tiger first evolved. Though tigers still roam the Siberian forests, their numbers are dangerously low. The chilly origins of the species have left their traces on the tigers that inhabit southern jungles. During the hottest parts of the years, southern tigers spend much of their time resting in the shade or cooling themselves in rivers. They are virtually the only cats to overcome what appears to be an instinctive dislike of water.

The ancestry of the tiger can be traced further back than these early Siberian fossils. About 36 million years ago there lived a small creature which was the ancestor of all modern cats. Known to scientists as *Dinictis*, this cat had a rather long body and canine teeth which were somewhat longer than in modern cats. It had evolved from civet-like ancestors which can

be traced back to about 60 million years ago.

From *Dinictis* arose two lines of cats. The first, referred to as stabbing cats, is no longer with us. In their time, the stabbing cats were the largest and most powerful carnivores on earth, culminating in the mighty sabre-tooth cat (*Smilodon*) which features so often in books about the prehistoric world. Though it is sometimes called the sabre-tooth tiger, *Smilodon* was only distantly related to the modern tiger.

The second evolutionary line goes by the name of biting cats. It produced all cats living today, including the tiger. Biting cats tend to kill their prey by using their powerful jaws to snap necks or to strangle. Stabbing cats, on the other hand, had weak jaws and relied on their long teeth to inflict fatal wounds.

Tigers are large cats, measuring up to 4m (13ft) in length depending on the subspecies. Their bodies are designed for their roles as hunters of large prey, a role for which the tiger is peculiarly well suited. The average tiger skull is some 35cm (14in) long and is powerfully constructed. The strong bones are designed to absorb the terrific forces exerted upon them by the impact of attack.

Coming in for most stress are, of course, the jaws. Depending on the size of prey, a tiger may either bite through the neck vertebrae or clamp its jaws around the throat and strangle its victim. For this reason the lower jaw is closed by powerful muscles, capable of exerting great pressure. The teeth are also well suited to the hunting role. The canines are much longer than the other teeth. During an attack these penetrate the flesh of the victim, enabling the tiger to gain a secure hold.

Once the prey has been killed, the tiger may use its canines to tear the carcass apart. In such instances the sharp claws are used to hold down the carcass while the teeth tear loose a lump of flesh. The claw-armed paws may also be used in hunting to disable

7

Unlike other big cats the tiger does not avoid water, but enjoys the cool streams during the mid-day heat.

running prey. The cheek teeth are generally used to slice through meat and tendons. These teeth meet like the blades of a pair of scissors, making them ideal for their purpose.

The muscular torso of the tiger is ideally suited to the task of bringing the ferocious teeth and jaws into action. The legs are strong and supple. When stalking, a tiger is able to sneak along low to the ground with a smooth, gliding motion. The legs can carry the weight of the tiger in almost any position required, and can hold the animal motionless if the prey becomes nervous.

In the last moments of the attack, the tiger's body becomes a fast-moving object of fluid speed. The tiger may pounce or run its quarry down depending on circumstances, and its muscular legs and remarkably sinuous backbone are able to carry the tiger to its destination.

The most noticeable feature of the tiger is, of course, its boldly striped coat. In a zoo or other unnatural surroundings the striped coat stands out as a beautiful and clearly defined fur.

These apparently rather startling markings are, however, part of the tiger's natural camouflage. The first purpose of the stripes is to break up the outline of the cat. The shape of a tiger is indelibly imprinted on the instincts of prey animals. When they see a tiger they sense danger and become nervous. The bold stripes help to disrupt this tell-tale outline. The stripes are particularly effective in the long grass which tigers frequent for they match the shadows cast by the upright stems.

The red-yellow background colour is also a camouflage mechanism. Much of the tiger's hunting activity takes place at dusk or dawn. In a hot sunny climate, as in India, sunsets and dawns flood the landscape with the rosy glow of the low-lying sun. In such light, the ruddy coat of the tiger is by far the best colour for blending into the background. The colour scheme is also suitable for night hunts. The dark shades of the coat blend in well with the forest shadows cast by moonlight.

The paws of the tiger are of great importance to the animal. The soft pads on which the tiger walks are very sensitive, allowing it to pick its way carefully across the forest floor without creating any noise. This very sensitivity can sometimes, however, be something of a drawback, for the tiger finds it difficult to negotiate sharp or

A tiger, having spotted a victim, slinks forward through long grass with its body held low to avoid detection. Its stripes will break up its outline in the vertical lines of the long grass.

9

uncomfortable surfaces. Tigers are known to be kept at bay by thorn fences and on several occasions they have been seen to avoid walking across bare rock baked hot by the midday sun.

The claws borne on the toes are as sharp and deadly as those of other large cats. Though preferring to kill with its jaws, the tiger occasionally lashes out with its razor-sharp claws to cripple or slow down a fleeing victim.

The pug marks left by the tiger's pads and claws are distinctive and can be used by trackers to determine the age and sex of the creature they are following. Some naturalists claim that individual tigers can be recognized from their pug marks. This has for a long time been the basis of estimates of tiger population in India. However, this task requires immense skill and great familiarity with the individual animals concerned.

In most of these physical characteristics, the tiger (*Panthera tigris*) is very like the lion (*Leo leonis*), though in behaviour they are very different. Indeed the behavioural divergence is so great that the two cats are never found together. The lion hunts on the plains, the tiger in the forests. Compared with cats other than the lion, the tiger's physical characteristics are very much more distinctive.

The only other large cat with which the tiger shares a range is the leopard (*Panthera pardus*). This creature is much more athletic, frequently climbing trees and buildings. The leopard often takes small prey, such as birds, though it is quite capable of tackling the larger prey preferred by tigers. Perhaps this liking for small prey enables the two carnivores to exist side by side. It is certainly true that leopards frequent the outskirts of villages and towns. They prey on domestic fowl and pet dogs together with larger farm animals. In such circumstances the leopard is a nuisance to man, but keeps out of the way of the tiger.

The exact nature of the relationship between tigers and leopards is not clear. A

10

A leopard resting in a tree. These cats often drop on to prey from tree branches. Tigers rarely, if ever, employ such tactics.

few hunters and foresters have seen cats of the two species cooperating in the hunt. However, it seems more likely that the great cats are rivals. More than once a leopard has been driven from a kill by the arrival of a tiger. One leopard was observed to run up a tree in panic and hide for more than an hour when the roar of an angry tiger came from close by.

Several smaller species of cat share the range of the tiger. The jungle cat (*Felis chaus*), golden cat (*Felis temmincki*), marbled cat (*Felis marmorata*) and leopard cat (*Felis bengalensis*) are all species slightly larger than the domestic variety. They live in a variety of habitats ranging from dense jungle to derelict human sites. They generally hunt small mammals and reptiles and so rarely come into conflict with the tiger in the search for food.

An oddity is the fishing cat (*Felis viverrina*). As its name suggests, this cat prefers to hunt fish in the swamps and estuaries where it makes its home. It is beautifully marked but rarely seen for its spotted coat renders it virtually invisible in the reeds and dappled sunlight of its habitat. The strangely uncat-like behaviour of this species is no longer considered to be taught to cubs by parents. A fishing cat kept in captivity almost from birth immediately began striking at fish when shown a river for the first time.

The cats that co-exist with the tiger live largely independent of their bigger cousin. Apart from, possibly, the leopard, they concentrate on prey the tiger would usually shun. The same cannot be said of the wild members of the dog family. Throughout much of its range the tiger lives alongside the wolf (*Canis lupus*). To some extent the two animals are kept apart by the wolf's preference for open country. However, the two animals share prey species and have sometimes come into competition.

In India the dhole (*Cuon alpinus*), or wild

Opposite above: The pug mark of an adult tigress photographed on a river bank in Nepal.

Opposite below: The pug marks of the increasingly rare Indian lion. The two great cats do not compete, because they inhabit different habitats.

Right: The rarely seen jungle cat which lives alongside the tiger, but which hunts smaller prey.

Below: A pack of wolves, which share the same prey as the tiger, but usually avoid clashes with the great cat.

dog, comes into much closer contact with the tiger. Both inhabit forested regions and prey on the same deer and pigs. The individual dhole is much smaller and weaker than the tiger, but its behaviour more than makes up for this deficiency. The dhole run in packs of up to 30 individuals. Each pack is headed by a recognized leader which coordinates the hunt and feeding activities.

The determination and unrivalled ruthlessness of the dhole packs make them feared by animals and hated by men. Once a hunt has begun, the dholes will run down their chosen prey across surprisingly long distances. The yaps and howls of the hunters desperately trying to coordinate their actions amid the dense undergrowth alert the inhabitants of the surrounding jungle to their presence. Eventually the prey, be it chital, boar or sambar, is dragged down. The dhole do not bother to kill the unfortunate victim before beginning to feed and rip out chunks of meat.

The enormous fear created by dhole has been witnessed many times. Old time game hunters knew that when a dhole pack arrived in an area they might as well go home and drink tea. The game hide in fear and it is beyond the skill of human hunters to find them. On several occasions deer being pursued by dhole have made a line for villages or work camps, their fear of man overridden by the terror inspired by the wild dogs.

These formidable predators are the only true rivals of the tiger. Not only do they compete for similar prey, they also come into direct confrontation. On many occasions dhole packs have come across a tiger on a kill. Sometimes one or the other has retreated after threats and shows of strength. In rare instances, however, a battle royal has ensued. The lone tiger relies on its superior strength, for it is capable of smashing a dhole skull with a single swipe of its claws. The dogs, meanwhile, use their greater numbers to divert the tiger and nip in for telling bites on the cat's flanks and hindquarters.

The terrific din set up by such fights can be heard for miles through the jungle and sends every creature scurrying for shelter. The angry roars of the tiger mingle with the yaps and barks of the dhole in an ear-splitting crescendo of noise. These battles seem to be fairly evenly matched. Sometimes the tiger is killed, but it usually manages to slaughter a few dhole in the struggle.

More peaceably associated with the tiger are the hyaena (*Hyaena hyaena*) and the jackal (*Canis aureus*). Indian hyaenas live singly in burrows deep in the jungle. Though they have been known to hunt, hyaenas rely on scavanging for most of their food. They usually only move on to tiger kills when the feline is absent, for a hyaena is no match for a tiger. On the few occasions when a tiger catches a hyaena stealing meat, it attacks. If the hyaena does not flee quickly enough it is usually killed outright.

Jackals likewise scavenge from tiger kills. They too run the risk of sudden death if they are discovered. Sometimes a jackal may make frequent, short visits to a carcass. On each trip it takes a chunk of meat and then retreats to devour it. In this way it spends as little time as possible in the dangerous vicinity of the kill.

It is into this complex picture of predators and scavengers that the tiger fits. There can be no doubt as to its position. The tiger is the greatest carnivore of them all. It hunts the largest prey and is capable of overpowering and controlling all other creatures in the forests. Only the Indian dhole can stand up to the tiger, and only then when having the strength of numbers. Though always occupying the dominant position, the role of the tiger varies slightly in its various habitats. The tiger ranges over such vast areas that there are differences not only in the landscape it inhabits but also in the various subspecies of tiger itself, and these are described in the next chapter.

Above: A pair of striped hyaenas; these animals frequently take meat from unguarded tiger kills.

Left: A lone jackal. Although able to hunt in their own right, jackals often scavenge from tiger kills.

13

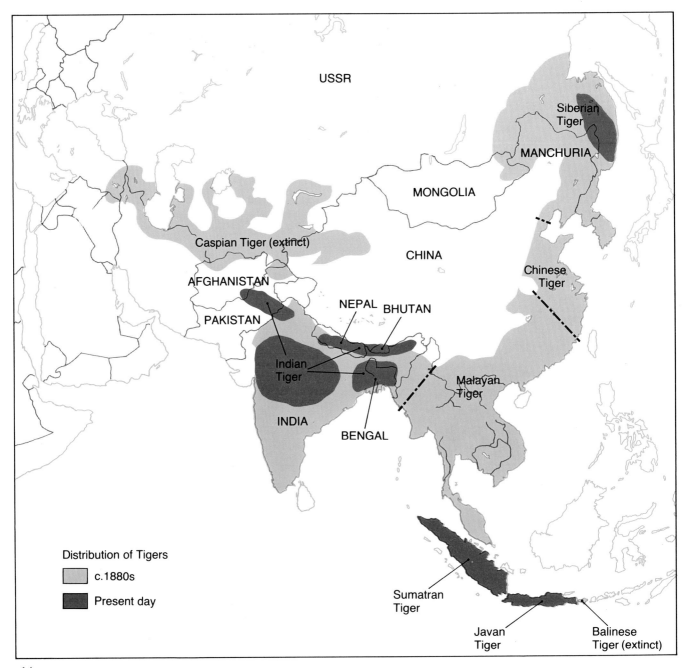

USSR

Siberian
Tiger

MANCHURIA

MONGOLIA

Caspian Tiger (extinct)

CHINA

Chinese
Tiger

AFGHANISTAN

NEPAL   BHUTAN

PAKISTAN

Indian
Tiger

Malayan
Tiger

INDIA

BENGAL

Distribution of Tigers

c.1880s

Present day

Sumatran
Tiger

Javan
Tiger

Balinese
Tiger (extinct)

The World of the Tiger

The tiger almost certainly first evolved in the cold northern forests of Siberia, and spread throughout Asia in Quaternary times (2 million years ago onward).

The actual movements of the tiger population remain something of a mystery. There are contrasting theories of how the tiger spread out to reach its present homes, but they basically hold to a standard pattern. Perhaps because of deteriorating climatic conditions, or because of population growth, the tigers began to filter out from their original home. To the north were the vast stretches of barren tundra where a forest hunter could not hope to survive. The tiger therefore infiltrated southwards, spreading out to both east and west as it did so. After a while the movement met the barrier presented by the impassable Himalayas and the Gobi Desert. One stream of tiger movement was diverted eastwards to Manchuria and Korea. The other branch passed west of the mountain barrier to enter Turkestan.

The western branch pushed southwards between the Caspian Sea and the forbidding mountains of Tibet until it reached Persia. It was almost certainly this western branch which later pushed into India. Exactly when this occurred is unknown. However, the total absence of tigers on Sri Lanka indicates that tigers had not arrived when that island separated from India. At whatever time the tigers arrived in India they found a forest habitat greatly to their liking and increased prolifically. Only the fierce heat of a noon summer sun has remained intolerable to tigers. Even after thousands of years of adaptation to the Indian climate, tigers still need to cool themselves in rivers and to lie in the shade when temperatures soar.

Meanwhile the eastern branch of the tiger movement advanced steadily southwards. Pushing across China they reached Indo-China and the Malaysian Peninsula. Even

An Indian tiger, most numerous of the subspecies, warily watches the photographer as it stalks across open ground.

the ocean did not halt the spread of the great cats. Tigers are noted swimmers and in some remote era swam the narrow Straits of Malacca to reach Sumatra. From there the tigers moved on to Java and Bali, together with several minor islands. The wider sea crossings to Borneo and Sulawesi proved too much for them though. They had reached the maximum limits of their range.

The hundreds of thousands of years over which this movement took place has allowed the tiger populations of the various areas to evolve regional characteristics. In perhaps eight regions the differences are great enough to warrant scientific classificiation into subspecies. Debate as to both the number and range of these subspecies has continued over the years, and remains in dispute. However, the general picture of tiger populations is fairly certain.

In the original tiger home lives the Siberian tiger (*Panthera tigris altaica*). This is the largest subspecies of all, measuring up to 4m (13ft) long and weighing several hundred pounds. The Siberian tiger is distinguished not only by its large size but also by its heavy build. The massive head, stocky hindquarters and long fur of the

The ruff, or mane, of the Chinese tiger can be seen clearly on this snow-bound specimen.

Siberian subspecies give it a distinctive profile. Also noticeable is the greater proportion of white in this tiger's coat, and the lighter shading of the background colour.

These features are almost certainly adaptations to the habitat in which the Siberian tiger lives. It is an established fact that creatures in cool climates tend to be larger and more bulky than similar creatures elsewhere. The reason for this is probably heat loss. Mammals generate their own internal heat to counteract cold and maintain body processes. This heat is lost through the skin. Such heat loss can be reduced by insulating fur, with which the Siberian tiger is plentifully endowed.

It is the increase in size which is crucial though, for this tends to reduce the proportion of skin surface area to body size. In turn this reduces heat loss. It is, therefore, an advantage for a animal inhabiting a cold area to be large, so long as there is enough food to support such a bulky creature. Conversely, warmer regions tend to produce smaller and more slender animals, for the increase in skin area which this entails aids the loss of body heat during periods of excessive heat.

The Caspian tiger (*P. t. virgata*) stalks through the Caucasus Mountains and Iran. This subspecies is slightly smaller than the Siberian tiger and is somewhat darker in colour. The belly of the Caspian tiger sports a long fringe of fur which hangs down between its legs. The species also has a rather pronounced ruff or mane around its neck.

The Indian tiger (*P. t. tigris*) is also a large animal, averaging perhaps 3m (10ft) in length. This subspecies is much shorter haired than the more northern subspecies and has a deeper, more richly coloured coat. The Indian tiger is by far the most numerous

The Sumatran tiger, noticeably smaller than most other subspecies, is now close to extinction on its island home.

information concerning tiger behaviour is derived from studies of the Indian tiger.

The eastern branch of the tiger family gave rise to rather more, though individually less numerous, subspecies. The Chinese tiger (*P. t. amoyensis*) has a smooth coat with narrower stripes and a stocky tail. Living to the south of the Chinese tiger is the Malayan tiger (*P. t. Corbetti*), which was named in honour of the famous Jim Corbett. This subspecies is noticeably slimmer and smaller than the Chinese variety. It roams through the dense jungles of not only Malaya but also Thailand, Burma and much of Indo-China.

Undoubtedly it was the Malayan tiger which swam the ocean straits to reach the islands of Indonesia. Long isolation on these islands has led to the development of subspecies on each island. The Javan tiger (*P. t. sondaica*), Sumatran tiger (*P. t. sumatrae*) and the Balinese tiger (*P. t. balica*) are all comparatively small creatures rarely more than 2.5m (8ft) in length. This lack of stature is not solely due to the hotter climates of the islands. Most island creatures are smaller than mainland counterparts. This general trend is due to the more limited food supplies available on islands. A creature with a less demanding appetite is better suited to survive in such conditions.

The astounding spread of the tiger throughout Asia was probably attained because of the tiger's territorial habits. For most of its life a tiger will live and hunt within a set territory. The size of this area may vary with the abundance of game or the age and sex of the tiger. However, in good hunting country an area of about 41km (16 square miles) might be average for a male.

This range is not exclusive. Tigers do not usually exclude other tigers from hunting within their range. Certainly tigers of differing sexes will happily co-exist. Even the ranges of same sex tigers tend to overlap to a great extent. All the same the tiger is a solitary animal and if two were to meet

of the various tigers. It lives in areas which are easily accessible and which for generations have been open to Western scientists and naturalists. For these reasons the Indian tiger is the best studied and most completely known subspecies. Most of the

unexpectedly violence might ensue. To avoid this, tigers have complicated "spacing mechanisms" which ensure that they are generally aware of where other individuals are at any given time. These mechanisms range from scent marks to vocal signals and build up into a highly complex pattern.

At times in its life a tiger will break from this pattern. The most common time for this to occur is during adolescence, though temporary food shortages may also break the system. When a tiger becomes too old to stay with its mother, it will wander off in search of a range for itself. Other tigers will tolerate these nomads while they move through their territory, so long as they do not linger too long. When the juvenile finds an area which is unoccupied or which is able to support it without competition with resident cats, it will settle down and establish a range. In this way the tiger population is constantly shifting and re-organizing itself. No doubt it was such juvenile nomads which spread southwards to carry their species across such vast territories from their origin in Siberia.

An Indian tiger drags a young deer into cover using the neck grip favoured for dealing with smaller prey.

Courtship and Cubs

Nobody who has ever been in close proximity to mating tigers will ever forget the experience. The noise is deafening and lasts for days. Yet the process begins quietly, even silently. As part of their spacing behaviour, designed to avoid unpleasant chance encounters, tigers spray scent on various objects. The scent is produced in a gland beneath the tail, and may be reinforced with a token urination. The objects most commonly chosen are trees and stumps. The act of spraying places the scent at the head height for a tiger, making it more likely that another will notice it. The smell persists for only a matter of hours and is intended to advertise the presence of a tiger, rather than mark its territory as would be the case for dogs.

When a tigress is in heat her spray alters in composition and this change can be detected by males. If there are no males in the area at the time the female becomes unreceptive and then repeats the cycle a few weeks later. If, however, a male is in the area and finds the spray he will follow the female, possibly calling to announce his presence.

A pair of tigers take a brief rest during the long and noisy mating progress.

Left: Love play, including rolling and licking, plays a large part in mating.

Below: At the actual moment of mating the tiger grips the tigress by the neck and emits a screeching noise. The pair will mate many times during courtship.

The female will reply and the two tigers eventually make contact in the dense undergrowth.

Upon meeting the tigers will pass through the usual procedure followed by tigers coming across each other. The make a facial expression known as *flemen*. This involves wrinkling the nose and protruding the tongue and may be connected with sensing smell. The potential mates then engage in a certain amount of play while they get to know each other and become certain of the other's intentions.

Once the preliminaries are over the noisy process of mating can begin. Throughout the process the tigers engage in a wide range of vocalizations. The tigress utters earthshaking roars at intervals, punctuated with quieter grunts. The tiger, meanwhile, prefers high pitched squeals and long moans. The cacophony can be amazing.

A mother tigress with two cubs only a few weeks old. At this age the cubs are totally dependent on their mother.

Tigers may mate several dozen times each day, and the process lasts for three days and nights. In this time the tigers do not hunt, but spend all their time in each other's company.

Once mating is over the pair separate. Though they may meet later, the male plays no role in finding food for the tigress nor in raising the offspring. Gestation lasts about 100 days and the tigress continues hunting almost up to the moment of birth. Wild tigers have never been observed giving birth, but it seems that the tigress finds a quiet, secluded place.

The actual process of birth is over remarkably quickly and usually occurs at night. Exhausted by the birth, the tigress lies on her side to allow the cubs to suckle. She gives them no help in finding the teats; the blind cubs tend to blunder around for some time before they find what they are searching for. The average size of a litter seems to be three, though as many as six or as few as one may be born. From the average litter of three it seems that one usually survives into adulthood.

Once the birth is over the tigress stays with her helpless, blind infants for some

When the mother tiger goes hunting she leaves her cubs hidden in undergrowth. If they are disturbed the cubs will call their mother, who returns to protect them.

ime. While they remain totally dependent he mother keeps the cubs carefully hidden. Every few days she will move the cubs to a new hiding place in case they are found by ackals or other scavengers. These precautions are especially necessary as the igress is alone and has no mate to help her.

When hunger impels her to hunt, the igress will leave the cubs at night for as hort a time as possible. She will make a kill, hide the carcass and eat as much as she requires before hurrying back to her young. During the daylight hours the mother stays with the cubs. At first, as much as three-quarters of the daylight hours may be spent n suckling, though this proportion declines rapidly.

After about a month the pattern changes. The mother tigress begins to eat more than he actually needs at the kill. When she returns to the cubs she regurgitates some of the meat in partly digested form. This introduces the cubs to solid food in a gentle, steady process. After a second month the tigress starts to bring lumps of meat to the cubs, which they devour. However, suckling continues, in reduced form, well into the third month of a cub's life.

Throughout the early months of the cubs' life the mother tigress is extremely protective and irritable. She will not tolerate other tigers close to the cubs' hiding place. More than one fatal struggle between tigers has been precipitated when one inadvertently intruded on a mother's territory. Under such circumstances spacing signals take on a new urgency.

It is not long before the mother tiger starts the cubs' training in hunting techniques. Perhaps the earliest schooling involves the mother twitching her tail while the cubs do their best to pounce and secure a hold. The cubs will also stalk and launch mock attacks on each other. In this way they are learning the essential skills of silent movement and lightning assaults.

The mother will soon be allowing the cubs to follow her for short distances at night. In the security of darkness the cubs learn the ways of the forest and the lay of the land around their home. By the age of six months the cubs are accompanying their mother on daytime trips as well. They learn the benefits of bathing in cool water during the heat of the day and continually practise their hunting skills.

At about the same age, the cubs are taken on their first hunts. Usually the mother will instal her young in a tangle of undergrowth where they will be safe from other predators. From here they are able to watch their mother pounce and kill a prey animal. The cubs remain hidden until the mother has subdued the victim and gives a soft grunt

Right: Mother with two cubs aged about 10 months. At this age the cubs accompany their mother on hunts and are allowed to take part in the kill itself.

Opposite: An 18-month-old female cub with its mother. Male cubs usually leave their mothers when aged around 14 months.

Then the cubs scamper out from hiding to join the feast.

By about the age of nine months the mother allows the cubs to launch attacks on small prey by themselves. The tigress, however, is always nearby to lend help if the cubs run into any trouble. Throughout this process of learning the tigress always puts the cubs' welfare ahead of her own. The young always eat first at a kill. The mother will rest nearby, keeping a wary eye open for danger. Only when the cubs have eaten their fill will the tigress move in to feed herself.

At the age of about a year the cubs are virtually full grown. The affectionate bond between them and their mother, however, remains fairly intact. In some cases mothers and cubs may remain in close contact for nearly two years. However the growing appetites and increasing agressiveness of the cubs generally leads to tensions well before this. Male cubs begin to wander off for short periods soon after their first birthday. The may go their own way at any age between 13 and 18 months. The daughters, however, tend to stay with the mother rather longer. It is not unusual to find a 20-month-old female still keeping company with its mother.

The final break up of the family unit leads to an unsettled period for the young. Usually the hunting grounds around their birthplace are already filled by resident tigers. The adolescents become nomad tigers, roaming at will across long distances. The tigers through whose territory these wanderers move are generally tolerant of the interlopers, so long as no face-to-face confrontation occurs.

The young will continue to roam until they find an empty range or an area where the game supply is great enough to support an extra tiger. The process may take many months. When the tiger has found a range on which to become established it can settle down and breed, producing cubs of its own, and so the pattern is repeated.

The Hunt

The tiger is the greatest predator of the Indian forests. It will kill virtually anything that it is able to catch, so no animal however small or fleet is safe. The forests and grasslands which the tiger haunts are dense tangles of vegetation where the solitary creature can lurk in wait for its prey.

The wild forests contain such valuable timber trees as teak and rosewood together with the sal and other species. In the north these form luxurious, evergreen stands which remain a mass of plants throughout the year. Elsewhere the vegetation is more dependent on the monsoon rains. After the June deluge the plants burst forth in a riot of growth which gradually subsides until the

A tiger resting in open woodland, but remaining alert for signs of passing game.

26

A fine pair of spotted chital, possibly the favourite prey of the Indian tiger.

following spring brings a dry, parched look to the land.

It is among these forests and grasslands that the prey of the tiger find their food and sustenance. Tigers will usually prefer to tackle large prey which will provide them with food for several days. In India large prey usually means a deer of one sort or another.

The largest of the Indian deer is the sambar (*Cervus unicolor*) which may stand 1.6m (5ft) at the shoulder and weigh over 300kg (650lb). Sambar move cautiously through the forest, being more active at night than during the daylight hours. Sambar are not herd animals. The stags lead solitary lives, except during the autumn rutting season, while the females may congregate in groups of about half a dozen.

Like the sambar, the chital (*Axis axis*) is found throughout India and much of Indo-China. The delicately patterned coat of this deer has earned it the name of "spotted beauty" and makes it instantly recognizable. The chital is at home both in forest and on grasslands, being able to eat both grass and leaves. It breeds prolifically and in suitable conditions can produce large numbers in remarkably short periods of time. Some tigers seem to have a preference for it, ignoring other potential victims when chital are nearby.

Sambar and chital both emit loud danger cries when they sense a tiger, thus warning other animals of the predator's presence. The hog deer (*Axis porcinus*), however, has a visual signal. When alarmed the hog deer raises its tail and flees. Beneath the tail is a

27

The muntjac hides in deep jungle and alerts the jungle to a tiger on the move with its curious alarm call, which sounds like a small dog barking.

white patch. Other hog deer seeing this alarm signal immediately set off in the same direction. Hog deer love to frequent riverside meadows, grazing in the lush grasses to be found there.

Somewhat rarer and less widely distributed is the barking deer or muntjac (*Muntiacus muntjac*). This small deer is extremely shy and is seen only infrequently, even in areas where it is common. The tiger, however, seems to have little trouble finding and killing this charming little creature.

The closely related antelope of India are also favoured prey. The largest of these is the nilgai (*Boselaphus tragocamelus*) or blue cow. The nilgai lives in forests, prefering more open country to the denser thickets. Congregating in small groups the nilgai present a tempting target for the tiger.

More formidable as victims are the wild cattle of India. The gaur (*Bos gaurus*) is related to the yak. It lives in dense forests, often in mountainous areas and the adults are tremendously strong animals. Equally powerful is the wild buffalo (*Bubalus bubalis*) which may weight up to 900kg (2,000lb). Wild buffalo rarely flinch from defending themselves with their sharp, long horns. When tackling such creatures, tigers generally prefer to avoid adults and choose calves or elderly animals. Tigers have also been known to take young elephants.

During the day, or when they are not hungry, tigers tend to rest as much as possible. They may lie in the shade, splash around in a river or simply doze. However, when hunger drives a tiger to hunt, its behaviour becomes very different. The hunt begins as the tiger stealthily makes its way through its range. If there are any sites, such as waterholes, where prey tend to gather, the tiger will visit these places. As it moves the cat keeps as quiet as possible so as to avoid startling any of the smaller animals which may give an alarm call and alert other creatures.

Sometimes a tiger will lie in wait beside a waterhole or a forest track. Such a strategy has the advantage that the tiger expends little energy searching for prey, it comes to him. It is also more likely that an attack, once launched, will be successful for the prey may approach a hidden tiger closer than a stalking tiger can approach a wary animal. However, the ambush technique is used little for there is no guarantee that any prey will use a particular path. Tigers usually have more success wandering through their territory, searching for victims.

When a suitable prey is sighted, the tiger ceases its wandering and studies the land. If the intended victim moves away, the tiger follows with slow, careful tread. If it is stationary the tiger will begin its approach. Tigers prefer to move through cover whenever possible. A hunting tiger approaches its target by a circuitous route which will place it in the open as little as possible. When open ground needs to be crossed, the tiger sinks down to keep its body close to the ground and moves forwards with a slow, gliding motion. Occasionally, a prey may sense the presence

An adult gaur feeding on open ground. Tigers usually avoid such large prey unless they can launch a surprise attack.

of the tiger and become nervous. If the animal does not flee, the tiger may halt its stalk and lie perfectly still. Sometimes tigers have been known to remain motionless like this for many minutes before resuming the hunt.

When the tiger has approached as close as it feels possible without detection it may lie still for a while. Gathering its legs under-

neath its body, the tiger readies itself for the final rush. In the final moments the hunter will bob its head as if trying to get a final indication of the distance to be covered. With an explosive burst of energy the tiger rushes forward at top speed. At the last moment the tiger may spring clear of the ground, hoping to bring the prey down by landing on top of it. Sometimes the tiger

needs to make a second spring to reach its victim. If the tiger does not make contact after a second spring the intended victim usually makes good its escape for the tiger is not capable of sustained speed.

The actual process of killing is largely determined by the angle of attack and the size of the prey. Whenever the chance presents itself, however, the tiger attempts a technique which may be called the neck grip. This involves the tiger placing its jaws across the top of the neck as close to the head as possible. The powerful jaw muscles can then be used to crush the vertebrae, severing the spinal cord and killing the victim. When this technique is used successfully a tiger can despatch even a large victim in about 30 seconds.

When attacking from behind, the tiger usually springs onto its prey, landing astride the back and reaching forwards to seize the throat. The head on attack is equally straightforward for the tiger which can usually force the prey creature's head down to expose the neck. Flank attacks can be more a problem, but an experienced tiger is usually able to secure a neck grip. Younger tigers may need to struggle to subdue a victim.

When a neck grip is not possible, tigers prefer to attack the throat. The sharp teeth of the tiger are likely to sever vital blood vessels. Even if the jugular is missed the tiger is quite capable of maintaining a strong grip long enough to strangle most animals.

Such swift, clean kills are typical of the tiger. It prefers a short, simple struggle to subdue its prey. This involves little risk of injury to the tiger and enables it to begin feeding as soon as possible. On occasion, however, the tiger is forced to abandon its usual clinical methods. If an intended victim is too large or powerful for a tiger to attack with confidence, the decision may be taken to disable it first. To do this the tiger will

Opposite: A tiger on the prowl. The russet coat and disruptive patterning of its coat makes the hunter nearly invisible to prey.

Left: A tiger sighting prey. The tiger lowers its body and raises its head so as to gain a clear view while taking advantage of whatever cover is available.

Once close enough to attack, the tiger bounds forwards at high speed. If it does not reach its target within a few seconds, the tiger will normally give up the hunt.

lash out with powerful swipes of its claws. Such a blow may sever a hamstring or bring a creature to its knees, thus laying it open to a more conventional attack. Such a method is often used against buffalo and gaur.

Having killed its prey the tiger generally follows a set pattern of feeding. First of all the tiger drags its kill to a spot where it will be safe from scavenging vultures and jackals. This may be in a tangle of undergrowth or beneath a rock. Then the tiger neatly cuts away the skin from the hindquarters of the carcass. Determined

tugging with teeth and claws strips the skin away to reveal the flesh beneath. This process can take as much as 30 minutes, after which the tiger may rest before eating.

An adult tiger is capable of eating some 28kg (60lb) of meat at a sitting. If the carcass contains more meat than this the tiger will return on subsequent nights. During the day, the tiger very often stays close to the carcass to guard it from others. The tiger not only devours the muscle of a kill, it also slits open the abdomen to find kidneys, lungs and other organs. Tigers may return to a carcass several nights running, even continuing to feed after the flesh has begun to putrefy.

Of the animals it is likely to encounter the tiger is usually prepared to make a meal of all except one. The exception is man, tigers, along with other creatures, having learnt that man is a dangerous opponent. There is also the fact that tigers do not come across many humans in the depths of the forest. When men are met on farmland or open country, the tiger is usually off its home range and uneasy. Despite this tigers have become notorious as man-eaters. It is a reputation which, to some extent, is deserved.

While the vast majority of tigers avoid man whenever possible, a few individuals take to man killing as a normal hunting technique. When tigers were still plentiful and common throughout their range, man-eating was a constantly recurring problem. Every few years a tiger would turn man-eater. Jim Corbett, who tracked down and killed many man-eaters earlier this century, became perhaps the greatest expert on this unusual and disconcerting phenomenon.

Corbett believed that man-eating tigers take to this alien diet usually because of injury. Several of the tigers he was called upon to shoot were found to have been disabled either due to porcupine quills in the foot or a hunter's bullet lodged in the body. Wounded in this way a tiger would find it very difficult to surprise and kill its normal prey. Deer and antelope are too alert and powerful to be killed by a crippled tiger. Lone humans, on the other hand, are generally less nervous and put up less of a fight. Such a fact is usually discovered accidently by the tiger. If a human disturbs

A pair of tigers sharing a kill. The victim is a young gaur. Adult tigers sometimes share kills, but such co-operation usually takes place between family groups.

The Maharajah of Panna scans the wild country of Madhya Pradesh for signs of tiger.

it, the beast may lash out and kill the human. Having achieved a kill the hungry tiger may feed. This will lead the animal to suppose that humans are easy prey and to begin its career as a man-eater.

The reign of a man-eater in earlier times was a terrible affair. The villagers went in fear of the beast and were frightened to leave their homes. Remote fields were untilled and nobody travelled jungle roads unless they had to. The agriculture and economy of the region could break down, bringing poverty and starvation in its wake. The villagers were generally unable to deal with a man-eater with the simple tools at their disposal. They relied upon the maharajahs or British officials, who owned rifles, to save them. The sheer scale of a man-eater problem is often ignored today. However, even in this century there have been man-eaters which have operated for years and have killed more than 200 people.

Modern naturalists have sometimes tried to dismiss the old accounts of man-eaters as fables. They have pointed out the human fear of powerful predators and suggested that the term "man-eater" was used as a convenient excuse for killing a tiger. Others have suggested that the deaths attributed to tigers were, in reality, murders and the tiger simply an alibi. However, the accounts of Corbett and others leave little doubt that man-eating tigers were a very real problem in the days when the tiger population was some 20 times as great as it is today. Those who have confidently stated that tigers do not attack and eat humans under any circumstances received an unpleasant shock when a wave of man-eating broke out in northern India in the early 1980s. These attacks are very different from those dealt with by Corbett and are part of the much larger problem of the human relationship with tigers.

Opposite: A lone tiger crosses a forest road. The invasion of the forest by man has led to violent clashes between the two species.

35

Decline of the Tiger

Before about 1750 humans had made little impact on the tiger population. The tiger was able to roam across the continent of Asia almost at will. Wherever there was vegetation to provide cover and prey to provide food, the tiger reigned supreme. Exactly how many tigers there were at this time is almost impossible to estimate, but it was probably well in excess of 100,000 of which 40,000 were in India. Today only some 4,000 survive. The decline of the tiger has been a long process, and with many contributory factors.

Until the mid-18th century human attitudes to the tiger were largely conditioned by circumstance. The tiger was an exceptionally large and powerful carnivore which occasionally turned man-eater. Moreover, the virgin forests were almost alive with the mighty animals. Nobody who lived in Asia can have been unfamiliar with tigers, any more than a modern European can be unfamiliar with foxes. They were a fact of life.

Under such conditions the tiger was regarded as a dangerous part of the fauna. It was to be avoided at all costs and, when possible, destroyed. Such were the numbers

A print of 1860 showing a native prince hunting tiger in his state. The princes were great hunters, some bagging over a thousand tigers in the course of their lives.

of tigers and the primitive nature of human weapons that the tiger was easily able to maintain its position.

However, the introduction of increasingly efficient firearms made tiger hunting a viable, rather than suicidal, pastime. Only the wealthy could afford expensive guns, and tiger hunting, or *shikar* as it became known, developed as an aristocratic sport. At the same time greatly increased trade with Europe led to a demand for the luxury woods of Indian forests. The felling of large areas of jungle caused a reduction in the habitat of the tiger. The first great assault on the tiger had begun.

As weapons technology improved together with the demand for timber and forest products, the tiger population took a terrible battering. By the later nineteenth century the total Indian population may have been reduced by half, perhaps more. The finger of blame for this decrease is today often pointed at the game hunters. These men, British officials and native aristocracy, looked on tiger hunting as the finest sport of all. It was held to demand great skill and coolness on the part of the hunter, who was very often in no little danger himself. In fact given the natural fear of man in the tiger and the increasingly sophisticated firearms available, the hunters were in little danger. All that was required was a steady hand and an efficient beating party.

With such advantages the hunters accounted for truly amazing numbers of tigers. The Maharajah of Sarguja, for instance, shot no less than 1,157 tigers in the course of his long life. In Nepal one *shikar* party despatched 39 tigers in 11 days.

In fact the depredations of the *shikar* parties may not have been solely responsible for the catastrkphic decline in tiger populations. It was in the interests of the aristocratic hunters to maintain a certain number of tigers so that there would always be fine hunting. To this end both British and local rulers tended to maintain forestry resources in the form of native forest. The

European hunters of 1807 hunt tigers Indian-fashion from elephant back. Such early hunting with inaccurate muskets made little impression on the numbers of tigers.

whole ecosystem of the jungle was maintained and harvesting carried out on a small scale, which would not overstep the ability of the forest to regenerate itself.

The peasant farmers, however, had other ideas. Their very lives depended on being able to raise enough food to feed themselves and their families. In order to stave off the famines which periodically swept India, the farmers needed to take advantage of all land possible. They felled large areas of virgin forest, depriving the tiger of its natural habitat. They had no compunction about eradicating large predators who were destroying valuable livestock, and poisoned meat was put out. Where figures are available it seems that the villagers killed about three times as many tigers as the sportsmen. When the damage to habitat is considered it seems clear that the spread of farmland caused more damage to the tiger population than hunting.

The twentieth century has seen a fatal combination of booming human population, technological advances and lack of foresight. The rapidly increasing numbers of humans in India need homes. For the vast majority of them this means a farm on which

A rare white tiger. Such albinos are most common around Rewa, whose native princes treated the rarities as prize specimens and kept them alive in a private zoo. When one white tiger died in the 1920s, it was stuffed and presented to the King-Emperor George V.

to carry on the traditional forms of agriculture. This has swallowed up vast areas of tiger country as forests have been felled and grasslands opened up to the plough. In those areas still under forest, technology has led to a fall in country actually suitable for tigers. Species of tree are planted for commercial rather than habitat reasons, resulting in a decline in the density of native wildlife per acre.

The effects of these developments on the tiger population of India was dramatic. In the early 1950s Jim Corbett, now an elderly man who had long since given up hunting, thought that there might be more than 2,000 tigers left alive. In 1972 a major government survey was carried out by men studying pugs and other information. They found that just 1,800 tigers were alive in India.

Throughout its range the tiger has experienced a similar fall in numbers. The Bali tiger is almost certainly extinct, as is the Caspian. The island of Java has been so heavily developed that tiger habitat seems incapable of supporting a viable population. Elsewhere the situation is rather better. About 600 tigers live on Sumatra. Indo-China supports a population of perhaps 2,000 tigers, though figures are difficult to come by. Population numbers for the Chinese tiger are even scarcer. The Siberian tiger seems to be restricted to only a part of its former range, principally in Manchuria and Sikhote, in the U.S.S.R. Despite this restriction, the tigers seem to be maintaining their numbers well and are unlikely to face extinction if their habitat is not encroached on further.

Opposite: An Indian tiger in its natural habitat of dense forest. The replacement of natural forest with managed commercial forests with little cover has been a factor in the decline of tiger numbers.

Preservation

One of the first to realize the desperate plight into which the tiger had fallen was Jim Corbett. As early as 1944 he wrote "a tiger is a large-hearted gentleman and when he is exterminated – as exterminated he will be unless public opinion rallies to his support – India will be the poorer by having lost the finest of her fauna."

Corbett worked ceaselessly to introduce conservation measures into forestry objectives and other government schemes. In large measure he was unsuccessful, for the public opinion of which he spoke did not believe that the tiger was in serious danger. Many who realized the plight of the tiger would not have been too sorry to see the great carnivore disappear. However, Corbett's work did pave the way for later generations of conservationists.

By the late 1960s the climate of opinion, at least in educated circles, was changing. The vital ecological role of the tiger was being recognized. Its killing of large herbivores, such as nilgai and boar, kept down the numbers of these animals to a manageable level. If it were not for the tiger the populations of these creatures would boom, stripping the forest of greenery and doing untold harm to the environment. It became recognized that the tiger benefitted the environment rather than harmed it, and should be preserved.

In 1969 the International Union for the Conservation of Nature (I.U.C.N.) passed a motion calling for the prohibition of tiger hunting throughout its range. It suggested that the poor countries which earned large amounts of money from *shikar* could make even more cash by organizing visits for tourists armed with cameras. Unfortunately, as yet nobody could state with certainty how many tigers were alive, nor to what degree they were endangered.

However, the Indian government, under Mrs Gandhi, responded swiftly. A total ban on tiger hunting was introduced and state governments given responsibility for preserving the tigers within their boundaries. The *shikar* companies and their workers protested about the ban, but the measure remained in force. Three years later came a watershed for the Indian tiger.

In 1972 S.R. Choudhury of the Department of Forests announced the results of his survey. He found that just 1,827 tigers remained alive in India. Choudhury himself

was to raise over one million dollars to aid in the preservation of the tiger. In fact the campaign raised nearly two million dollars in just 18 months. It also achieved a great deal by raising public awareness of the tiger situation.

Partly as a result of this activity the Indian government launched Project Tiger, which was designed to safeguard the future of what was now India's national animal. The aim of Project Tiger was to set aside certain areas of land which still offered ideal tiger habitat and to use them to maintain a viable breeding stock of tigers. A special commission was set up to discover how best this could be done with the resources available.

On 1 April 1973 Project Tiger came into operation under the chairmanship of Dr Karen Singh, a noted national politician. It

Left: A machan, or artificial platform, in the Sunderbans National Park. Such structures are used as observation and photographic platforms.

Below: Pug marks, on which most surveys of tiger population are based, are recorded by taking casts in plaster of Paris which can then be stored indefinitely for future reference.

admitted that the survey was bound to be rather inaccurate due to the secretive nature of tigers. Some conservationists suggested the methods used by Choudhury would produce rather optimistic results. They maintained that the true figure might be closer to 1,200. In the same year the I.U.C.N. drew up an international treaty which banned the export or import of any animal, skin or other products of a creature mentioned in their Red Book of endangered species. A great many countries signed the treaty, thus robbing poachers of a market for tiger skins.

But perhaps the most important development of 1972 was the launch of Operation Tiger. This was the brainchild of Guy Mountfort and his team at the World Wildlife Fund. The aim of Operation Tiger

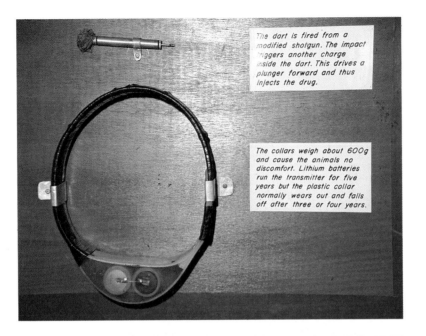

The dart is fired from a modified shotgun. The impact triggers another charge inside the dart. This drives a plunger forward and thus injects the drug.

The collars weigh about 600g and cause the animals no discomfort. Lithium batteries run the transmitter for five years but the plastic collar normally wears out and falls off after three or four years.

was appropriate that the project be launched in Corbett National Park, which had been named in honour of Jim Corbett and was located near his old home. Eight other national parks were included in Project Tiger: Manas, Palamau, Similipal, Ranthambhor, Kanha, Melghat, Bandipur and the Sunderbans. A tenth, Periyar, has since been added.

The policy of Project Tiger has been described as "do nothing and allow no one else to do anything". This is not as complacent as it may sound and is, in fact, an extremely dynamic and demanding task. The ideal is that within the tiger reserves no human activity should be allowed at all. The natural balance should be allowed to reassert itself. The tiger stands at the pinnacle of the food chain. Only by maintaining large areas of the habitat entire can the future of the tiger be guaranteed.

To this end the early years of Project Tiger were marked by large scale and energetic measures. Villages which intruded on the reserves were moved to other areas. Farmers were moved from their homes and given new land elsewhere. Forest harvesting was halted and all human intrusions energetically discovered and halted by forest rangers. In all, some 12,000 km² (4,600 square miles) of forest and other land has been set aside under Project Tiger.

It was hoped that these untouched reserves would act as core areas for the recovery of the tiger populations. Within the reserves tigers could breed naturally, building up their numbers and producing a surplus. The surplus, it was hoped, would move out of the core areas to find new homes during their juvenile nomad period. The new homes would be in the less protected, but still suitable forest areas under human management. The core areas would thus act as a reservoir of tiger population.

On the whole the policy seems to be working. Between 1972 and 1978 the tiger population of the core areas is estimated to

Left: A drugged tiger being measured and tagged by National Park personnel as part of Project Tiger.

Opposite above: A tranquilizer dart and radio collar used during tiger studies in Nepal.

Opposite below: Some park wardens prefer to record tiger pug marks by tracing their outlines on paper. This is not as accurate as taking plaster casts, but is quicker and cheaper.

have risen from 258 to about 500. Elsewhere in India the prohibition of *shikar* and greater concern for the tiger generally has led to a steady increase in the tiger population. Exactly how great this rise has been is difficult to estimate accurately. The total population of the Indian tiger may today be anywhere between 2,500 and 4,000. One problem in estimating numbers is that no rigorous species-wide survey has been conducted in recent years. Estimates rely on collating isolated local surveys and extrapolating these figures to other areas. One thing can be said with confidence, however,

Right: Officials of
Project Tiger
comparing pug marks
in an attempt to count
tigers in a small area
of India.

there are several hundred more tigers living wild today than in 1972.

The increase in the tiger population, however, has led to problems. One of the most dramatic is the number of man-eaters, small but increasing, which have become active. Such outbreaks appear to be localized, though they may involve several tigers in a short space of time. The reason for this is the greater number of villagers following the traditional Indian system of agriculture. This means that many more people are moving through the forests searching for firewood or grass, and young active tigers are losing their fear of them. At the same time increasing use of crops such as sugar cane, which provide ideal cover for tigers, encourage them to approach close to villages. The tigers are thus becoming accustomed to the sight and smell of humans as part of the environment, rather than dangerous interlopers which it is wise to avoid.

At the moment man-eaters are shot out of hand. This system worked when they were rogue individuals, but it cannot be thought of as a long-term answer. Perhaps the best solution would be to curtail the growing of certain crops in tiger country and to strengthen still further the controls on entry into tiger reserves.

Great efforts to save the tiger are also being made by conservationists in countries other than India. The Siberian tiger is protected in three reserves which between them have a population of some 400 animals. The Sumatran and Malayan tiger are also benefiting from protection measures. Though the future of a creature as rare and ecologically frail as the tiger can never be said to be safe, it does seem to have a fighting chance.

Opposite: The graceful
sleekness of the tiger
is perfectly shown in
this well-fed animal.

Index